AJACCIO

TRAVEL GUIDE

2023-2024

The Ultimate Guide to Top Attractions, Things to do, Itinerary, Best Activities, Accommodation (Hotels) Foods (Restaurants) Culture and History of Ajaccio

HENRY WAYNE

Copyright 2023 by Henry Wayne . All rights reserved. No part of this publication may be reproduced, or transmitted in any form or by any means including photocopying, recording or other electronic or mechanical methods, without the prior written of the publisher

TABLE OF CONTENT

INTRODUCTION..5
  About Ajaccio (Ajaccio's History and Culture)............... 5
  Geography and Climate..9
  Getting Around.. 15

CHAPTER 1: TOP ATTRACTIONS......................... 18
  Napoleon Bonapartes Birthplace................................ 18
  Parc des Iles Sanguinaires.....................................21
  Ajaccio Cathedral... 24
  Fesch Museum..27
  Sanguinaires Islands Sunset................................... 30

CHAPTER 2: LOCAL CUISINE............................33
  Corsican Delicacies...33
  Must-Try Restaurants.. 36
  Ajaccio's Best Cafe's... 39

CHAPTER 3: ACTIVITIES................................42
  Beaches and Watersports.......................................42
  Hiking Trails...49
  Boat Tours.. 52
  Ajaccio's Vibrant Nightlife...................................57

CHAPTER 4: DAY TRIPS..61
    Scenic Drive to Calanques de Piana............................. 61
    Visit to Bonifacio.. 64
    Wine Tasting in the Corsican Vineyards........................67

CHAPTER 5: SHOPPING...71
    Ajaccio's Markets... 71
    Unique Souvenirs... 75
    Boutiques and Local Crafts... 79

CHAPTER 6: PRACTICAL INFORMATION........... 82
    Accommodation Options... 82
    Transportation Tips... 86
    Safety and Health..90

CHAPTER 7: LANGUAGE AND COMMUNICATION.. 94
    Useful Phrases.. 94
CONCLUSION... 99

INTRODUCTION

About Ajaccio (Ajaccio's History and Culture)

Nestled on the southwestern coast of the French island of Corsica, Ajaccio is a city with a rich history and a dynamic culture that reflects its distinctive combination of French and Corsican influences. This Mediterranean treasure, birthplace of the legendary French Emperor Napoleon Bonaparte, has a rich tapestry of historical events and cultural traditions that make it a fascinating destination for visitors and history aficionados alike.

Historical Overview: Ajaccio's history extends back to ancient times when it was colonized by many Mediterranean civilizations, notably the Romans and Greeks. However, its evolution into a prominent urban center began in the late 15th century while it was under the jurisdiction of the Republic of Genoa. During this era, the city's defences were reinforced, and it became an important strategic port.

The city's most renowned historical person, Napoleon Bonaparte, was born in Ajaccio in 1769. Although he would go on to become one of the world's most legendary military leaders and monarchs, his early life in Ajaccio left an everlasting effect on the city's identity. Visitors may visit

Maison Bonaparte, the house where he was born, which is now a museum devoted to his life and legacy.

Cultural Fusion: Ajaccio's culture is a unique combination of Corsican and French elements. The Corsican identity is profoundly embedded in the city's culture, with the Corsican language (Corsu) being commonly spoken alongside French. Traditional Corsican music, famed for its melancholy polyphonic chants and the use of unusual instruments like the Corsican bagpipes (cetera), may be heard throughout the city.

Corsican cuisine is another cultural feature, with a focus on locally obtained delicacies like as shellfish, game, and fragrant herbs. Some must-try meals are "aziminu," a shellfish soup, and "figatellu," a sort of Corsican sausage. Visitors may savour these gastronomic pleasures at tiny, family-run restaurants known as "auberges."

Architectural Heritage: The cityscape of Ajaccio displays its rich past. Stroll through the narrow cobblestone alleyways of the old town, where you'll see colorful houses embellished with wrought iron balconies and attractive courtyards. The 16th-century Cathedral of Notre-Dame-de-l'Assomption is a stunning example of Genoese Baroque architecture and is a must-visit for its magnificent interior.

The city is also home to various sculptures and monuments devoted to Napoleon, notably the spectacular Place Foch statue. The Maison Bonaparte, aside from its historical value, is a well-preserved example of Corsican townhouse architecture from the 18th century.

Festivals and Traditions: Ajaccio holds a number of festivals and cultural events throughout the year. One of the most notable is the "Fête de Napoléon," held on August 15th, which honors Napoleon's birthday with parades, reenactments, and fireworks. The city also promotes Corsican customs at events like the "Fiera di u Vinu," a wine fair, and the "Fiera di a Castagna," a chestnut festival.

Natural Beauty: Beyond its history and culture, Ajaccio enjoys breathtaking natural beauty. The city is bordered by magnificent beaches with crystal-clear seas, making it a favorite destination for sun-seekers. The surrounding Corsican mountains provide options for trekking and exploring lush woods and challenging terrain.

In conclusion, Ajaccio is a city that easily integrates its rich history, distinct cultural legacy, and natural beauty. Whether you're interested in digging into the life of Napoleon Bonaparte, relishing Corsican cuisine, or simply basking in the Mediterranean heat, Ajaccio has something to offer every tourist. It's a location where history and culture come alive against a backdrop of stunning surroundings, making it a genuinely wonderful trip.

Geography and Climate

Geography

Certainly, let's dig into a deep investigation of the geography of Ajaccio, the capital city of Corsica, which is noted for its spectacular natural landscapes and distinctive geographical features.

Location and Overview: Ajaccio is situated on the western coast of Corsica, the fourth-largest island in the Mediterranean Sea. It is the largest city on the island and serves as its administrative and cultural center. The city is perfectly positioned between the rugged Corsican mountains and the peaceful shores of the Mediterranean, making it a tempting destination for both nature enthusiasts and history fans.

Geographical Features:

Coastline: Ajaccio features a gorgeous coastline that runs for around 20 kilometers (12 miles). This coastline is lined with a variety of gorgeous beaches, rocky coves, and picturesque bays. Some of the most popular beaches include Plage de Capo di Feno, Plage d'Argent, and Plage de Ricanto. The beautiful Mediterranean seas along the coast offer many options for water sports and passive swimming.

Mountains: To the east of Ajaccio, the Corsican mountains rise significantly. These mountains are an offshoot of the larger mountain range known as the Corsican Alps. Notable peaks in the neighborhood include Monte Gozzi and Monte d'Oro. These rocky mountains not only provide a stunning backdrop to the city but also offer fantastic hiking and outdoor adventure options for guests.

Valleys and Rivers: The Gravona River flows near Ajaccio, weaving its way through a lovely valley. The Gravona Valley is recognized for its lush foliage, beautiful towns, and natural splendor. It's a popular resort for visitors interested in discovering Corsica's natural scenery. Additionally, the Prunelli River and its valley are also close, contributing to the region's natural variety.

Islands: Ajaccio is bordered by numerous tiny islands, the most notable of which are the Îles Sanguinaires (Bloody Islands). These islands are noted by their red granite cliffs, spectacular vistas, and distinctive flora and wildlife. They are also a recognized natural reserve, giving them a refuge for birdwatchers and wildlife enthusiasts.

Natural Reserves: Beyond the Îles Sanguinaires, Ajaccio and its neighboring surroundings feature various natural reserves and protected areas. These include the Scandola Nature Reserve and the Calanques de Piana, both listed as UNESCO World Heritage Sites. These areas are home to magnificent geological structures, rich animals, and pure Mediterranean ecosystems.

Climate: Ajaccio boasts a Mediterranean climate, typified by moderate, rainy winters and hot, dry summers. The city benefits from its closeness to the Mediterranean Sea, which helps reduce temperature extremes and adds to the general pleasant environment.

In essence, Ajaccio's topography is a compelling combination of coastal beauty, rocky mountains, rich valleys, and attractive islands. This distinctive environment has contributed to the city's attraction as a year-round destination for those seeking natural beauties, outdoor sports, and a taste of Corsican culture. Whether you're interested in discovering the city's rich history, trekking in the mountains, or lazing on beautiful beaches, Ajaccio offers a broad selection of adventures within its gorgeous geographical background.

Climate

Ajaccio, located on the gorgeous island of Corsica in the Mediterranean Sea, features a distinct and appealing environment that is affected by its geographical location, proximity to the sea, and Mediterranean traits. The city's climate may be best defined as Mediterranean, affording inhabitants and visitors a pleasant and moderate atmosphere throughout the year.

Seasonal Variations: Ajaccio experiences various seasons, with each one bringing its own set of attractions and activities.

1. Spring (March to May): Spring in Ajaccio is a beautiful period of the year when the city comes alive with vivid flowers. Temperatures during this season range from 12°C (54°F) in March to 20°C (68°F) in May. The Mediterranean environment means that rain is rather infrequent, and the island starts to blossom with beautiful wildflowers.

2. Summer (June to August): Summer is the biggest tourist season in Ajaccio, and for good reason. The weather is bright and pleasant, with temperatures average approximately 27°C (81°F) in June and peaking to about 30°C (86°F) in July and August. The sea becomes invitingly warm for swimming, and outdoor activities such as hiking and water sports grow.

3. Autumn (September to November): Autumn is a beautiful season to visit Ajaccio, since the summer crowds clear away, and the weather remains good. Temperatures start to progressively decline from an average of 27°C (81°F) in September to roughly 20°C (68°F) in November. This is also the harvest season for Corsican grapes, giving it a fantastic opportunity to tour the local vineyards.

4. Winter (December to February): Winter in Ajaccio is mild compared to many other places of Europe. The temperatures stay about 12°C (54°F) throughout the day, while it seldom drops below 5°C (41°F) at night. While not as warm as the other seasons, it's still a wonderful time to explore the city without the summer throng.

Mediterranean Influence: The Mediterranean Sea plays a crucial impact in defining Ajaccio's climate. Its closeness guarantees that the city has a marine environment characterized by moderate temperatures and generally mild winters. The sea also has a moderating influence, reducing excessive temperature changes.

Rainfall: Ajaccio experiences most of its rainfall during the winter months, with December being the wettest. However, even during the wettest months, the city does not get considerable rainfall compared to many other places. This comparatively little precipitation contributes to the city's adaptability for outdoor activities year-round.

Microclimates: Corsica, in general, is recognized for its microclimates. The island's steep terrain generates changes in climate, with coastal parts like Ajaccio being warmer and wetter than the interior, which endures more significant temperature shifts.

In conclusion, Ajaccio's climate is a key appeal for travelers, delivering a wonderful mix between warmth and mildness throughout the year. Whether you like the boisterous summer ambiance or the peacefulness of the offseason, Ajaccio's Mediterranean environment provides a great experience for all seasons.

Getting Around

Getting about Ajaccio, the lovely capital city of Corsica, is rather uncomplicated because to its modest size and well-developed transit alternatives. Whether you're touring the city itself or utilizing it as a base for exploring the lovely island of Corsica, here's a guide on how to get about Ajaccio:

1. Walking: The city center of Ajaccio is pedestrian-friendly, making walking one of the finest ways to explore its picturesque streets, ancient landmarks, and seaside promenades. Most of the city's principal attractions, including the Napoleon Bonaparte House and Museum, the Fesch Palace, and the Old Town, are within easy walking distance of one other.

2. Bicycles: Biking is a popular and eco-friendly method to move about Ajaccio. The city offers multiple bike rental businesses, and there are designated bike lanes and trails along the seafront and in several other places. It's a terrific opportunity to appreciate the coastline views and explore the area at your own speed.

3. Public Transportation: Ajaccio has a dependable network of buses that connect various regions of the city and its suburbs. The buses are run by the Muvistrada firm, and you can obtain information about routes, timetables, and rates at the bus terminals or online. Public transportation is a cheap choice for moving about the city.

4. Taxis: Taxis are widely accessible in Ajaccio and may be hailed on the street or ordered in advance. They are a perfect alternative if you want a private and hassle-free way of transportation. However, they might be somewhat pricey compared to public transit.

5. Rental Cars: If you wish to explore Corsica beyond Ajaccio, hiring a car is a smart solution. Several rental vehicle businesses operate in the city and at the Ajaccio Napoleon Bonaparte Airport. Keep in mind that parking in the city center might be problematic during busy tourist seasons.

6. Ferries: If you're wanting to visit other regions of Corsica or surrounding islands, Ajaccio's port provides regular ferry connections. These boats connect Ajaccio to places including Porto-Vecchio, Calvi, and Sardinia. It's a wonderful approach to enjoy the Mediterranean and reach neighboring attractions.

7. Trains: Ajaccio has a train station, Gare d'Ajaccio, which connects the city to other areas of Corsica. The train system offers a unique opportunity to discover the island's gorgeous scenery, especially whether you're planning day trips or longer adventures.

8. Scooters and Electric Scooters: Scooter rentals, especially electric scooters, have grown increasingly popular in Ajaccio. They provide a flexible and efficient form of

transportation, especially for short excursions inside the city.

Overall, Ajaccio offers a choice of transportation alternatives to meet varied interests and needs. Whether you like to explore on foot, bike, or by using public transit, you'll find that moving around this lovely Corsican city is quite straightforward and fun.

CHAPTER 1: TOP ATTRACTIONS

Napoleon Bonapartes Birthplace

Napoleon Bonaparte's birthplace is a famous historical landmark located in Ajaccio, Corsica, France. This well-preserved ancient building, known as "Maison Bonaparte" or the Bonaparte building, retains enormous significance since it was the birthplace of one of the most prominent individuals in European history, Napoleon Bonaparte, who would later become Emperor of the French.

History: Maison Bonaparte was erected in the 17th century and was the house of the Bonaparte family. It was here, on August 15, 1769, that Napoleon Bonaparte was born. At the time of his birth, Corsica was still an autonomous republic, although it would subsequently become a part of France.

Architecture: The architecture of Maison Bonaparte is typical of Corsican townhouses of that era. It displays a classic Genoese façade, defined by its delicate pink and gray tones, wooden shutters, and wrought-iron balconies. The home has three levels and a courtyard, and it is designed in a rectangle shape with a central corridor.

Museum: Today, Maison Bonaparte has been turned into a museum dedicated to the life and times of Napoleon Bonaparte. It provides visitors a full look into Napoleon's early years and his family's background. The museum showcases a magnificent collection of antiquities, furniture, papers, and memorabilia linked with the Bonaparte family.

Highlights of the Museum:

Napoleon's Birth chamber: The focus of the museum is Napoleon's birth chamber, restored to look as it did in the 18th century. Visitors may view the basic cradle, antique furnishings, and the same bed where Napoleon was born.

Family Portraits: The museum contains various portraits of Napoleon's family members, offering background and insights into the family's social position and relationships.

Historical Documents: Visitors may study a collection of historical documents, including letters, maps, and official papers, providing light on Napoleon's early schooling and military training.

Napoleon's Early Life: Exhibits record Napoleon's upbringing and boyhood in Corsica, his study at the military college in mainland France, and his early military career.

grounds: Maison Bonaparte also features wonderful grounds where you may roam and observe the lush foliage and Mediterranean flora.

Visitor Experience: Visiting Maison Bonaparte is like going back in time to see the modest beginnings of a man who would go on to transform the geography of Europe. The museum delivers an entire experience, presenting not only historical items but also a knowledge of the cultural and political backdrop of Corsica in the 18th century.

Location: Maison Bonaparte is strategically placed in the centre of Ajaccio, making it easily accessible to travelers touring the city. Its central position allows visitors to combine a visit to the birthplace with other surrounding sites, like the Ajaccio Cathedral and the old town's attractive streets.

In conclusion, Maison Bonaparte is a must-visit for history aficionados and anybody interested in the life and legacy of Napoleon Bonaparte. It gives a unique opportunity to understand the early years of one of the most significant men in global history while experiencing the beauty of Corsican architecture and culture.

Parc des Iles Sanguinaires

Parc des Îles Sanguinaires, often known as the Islands of Blood, is a spectacular natural and cultural site located near the coastal town of Ajaccio on the French island of Corsica in the Mediterranean Sea. This archipelago comprises of four main islands, each with its own particular beauty and history. Here, we'll look into the beauty and significance of Parc des Îles Sanguinaires:

1. Natural Beauty: The Islands of Blood are famous for their outstanding natural beauty. These rocky islands rise steeply from the crystal-clear seas of the Mediterranean, producing a stunning and rough coastline environment. The peculiar red granite formations give the islands their distinguishing name, since "Sanguinaires" translates to "bloody" in French, reflecting the scarlet tint of the cliffs, especially after sunset.

2. gorgeous Sunsets: One of the major attractions of the Parc des Îles Sanguinaires is the ability to view gorgeous sunsets. As the sun drops below the horizon, the sky turns into a pallet of brilliant oranges and reds, throwing a warm and mystical glow over the islands. Many travelers and residents congregate here in the evenings to see this natural show.

3. Flora and Fauna: The islands are not simply a delight for the eyes but also a paradise for animal aficionados and botany lovers. The Mediterranean climate of Corsica has

nourished a unique environment on these islands, boasting a diversity of plant species, including native maquis flora. The islands are also home to seabirds, making it a popular place for birding.

4. Historic Lighthouse: One of the islands, Île de Mezzu Mare, is home to the Sanguinaires Lighthouse (Phare des Sanguinaires), a historic and iconic monument that has been directing sailors safely along the Corsican coast for generations. Visitors may examine the lighthouse's architecture and learn about its maritime history.

5. Walking and Hiking paths: Parc des Îles Sanguinaires has a network of well-maintained walking and hiking paths that allow visitors to explore the islands' rocky topography and enjoy panoramic views of the Mediterranean Sea. The routes are of varied difficulty levels, making it accessible to both casual strollers and more adventurous hikers.

6. Cultural value: Apart from their natural attractiveness, the Islands of Blood contain cultural value as well. They have been the inspiration for various painters, authors, and poets over the years. The islands have also been referenced in different works of literature, contributing to their cultural heritage.

7. Access: To visit Parc des Îles Sanguinaires, you may take a short boat excursion from Ajaccio's harbor, which adds to the experience and allows you to view the islands from the

water. The boat trip gives wonderful views of the Corsican coastline and the islands before you disembark to explore.

In conclusion, Parc des Îles Sanguinaires is a natural and cultural jewel on the island of Corsica. Whether you're drawn to its breathtaking landscapes, wildlife, maritime history, or simply seeking a tranquil location to watch the sunset, this archipelago provides a remarkable experience that encapsulates the essence of Corsican beauty and history.

Ajaccio Cathedral

The Ajaccio Cathedral, also known as the Cathedral of Our Lady of the Assumption (Cathédrale Notre-Dame-de-l'Assomption), is a spectacular ecclesiastical building located in the centre of Ajaccio, the capital city of Corsica, France. This medieval cathedral is not simply a place of prayer but also a notable architectural and cultural monument. Here is a full summary of the Ajaccio Cathedral:

History: The Ajaccio Cathedral has a rich history that reaches back to the 16th century. It was initially built in the Gothic architectural style, but over the centuries, it underwent several repairs and adjustments, including aspects of different architectural styles, including Baroque and Neoclassical. The cathedral is on the site of an ancient church and has played a significant role in the religious life of Ajaccio and Corsica.

Architecture: The cathedral's architectural design is a unique combination of elements due to its lengthy history of building and repair. The façade of the church is a superb example of Baroque architecture, containing ornate decoration, sculptures, and a magnificent entryway. The inside of the cathedral, however, shows a more Neoclassical design, with its clean lines, graceful columns, and a sense of space.

Interior Highlights: Inside the Ajaccio Cathedral, visitors are greeted to a quiet and dignified ambiance. Some prominent interior highlights include:

Altar: The high altar is a main element of the cathedral, displaying a stunning Neoclassical design with columns and a large crucifix.

Choir: The choir space is filled with beautiful woodwork and religious artwork, giving a calm atmosphere for worship and reflection.

Paintings: The cathedral has numerous excellent paintings, including religious scenes and portraits of saints, adding to the aesthetic and spiritual aura.

Napoleon's Baptismal Font: One of the most notable elements of the Ajaccio Cathedral is the baptismal font where Napoleon Bonaparte was baptized on July 21, 1771. This historical item attracts people from throughout the world.

Chapels: The cathedral features many chapels devoted to different saints, each with its own unique design and religious importance.

Napoleon Bonaparte link: The Ajaccio Cathedral is of great importance to history buffs owing to its link to Napoleon Bonaparte. As said, Napoleon was christened in this cathedral, and his family had a unique bond with the church. The church also holds mementos relating to the Bonaparte family, adding to its historical relevance.

Visitor Experience: Visitors to the Ajaccio Cathedral may appreciate both its religious significance and its historical and architectural splendor. It gives a calm getaway from the busy streets of Ajaccio and offers an insight into Corsica's complicated past, where religion and politics clashed.

Location: The cathedral's prominent location in Ajaccio makes it conveniently accessible for tourists touring the city. It is situated within walking distance of various attractions, including Maison Bonaparte, the Fesch Palace, and the historic old town.

In essence, the Ajaccio Cathedral is a compelling combination of architectural styles and historical relevance. Whether you're drawn to its artistic riches, its place in Corsican history, or simply want a moment of reflection, a visit to this gorgeous cathedral is a wonderful experience when touring Ajaccio and the island of Corsica.

Fesch Museum

The Fesch Museum, formally known as the "Musée Fesch - Palais Fesch des Beaux-Arts," is a notable art museum located in Ajaccio, Corsica, France. Named for its creator, Cardinal Joseph Fesch, the museum is known for its remarkable collection of European paintings, sculptures, and other artworks. Here's a thorough summary of the Fesch Museum:

History: The Fesch Museum has an interesting history related to its creator, Cardinal Joseph Fesch. Cardinal Fesch was a French diplomat and cleric who was also the maternal uncle of Napoleon Bonaparte. In the early 19th century, he acquired a great art collection, which he gave to the city of Ajaccio upon his death in 1839. The Fesch Museum officially opened its doors to the public in 1850.

Architectural Significance: The museum is situated in a superb Neoclassical structure known as the Palais Fesch. This architectural jewel was created in the late 1820s and early 1830s, giving an appropriate backdrop for the art collection it contains. The façade of the museum has Ionic columns and a grand entryway, giving it a beautiful and dignified aspect.

Art Collection: The Fesch Museum's collection is its principal attraction, containing a large and diverse selection of artworks. Some of the highlights of the museum's collection include:

European Paintings: The museum features a wonderful collection of European paintings, covering diverse periods and genres. It features paintings by prominent painters such as Titian, Botticelli, Veronese, and Delacroix. The collection comprises religious art, portraits, landscapes, and historical subjects.

Sculptures: In addition to paintings, the Fesch Museum holds a notable collection of sculptures, including Roman and Renaissance items. These sculptures give insight into the progression of sculptural methods and styles.

Decorative Arts: The museum also shows a range of decorative arts, including furniture, ceramics, and other objects from different periods.

Napoleonica: Given Cardinal Fesch's familial connection to Napoleon Bonaparte, the museum naturally contains a section dedicated to Napoleonica. This comprises photographs and artifacts relating to the Bonaparte family, offering historical background to Corsica's links with the French Empire.

Visitor Experience: Visiting the Fesch Museum is a voyage through the rich artistic heritage of Europe. The carefully organized collection allows visitors to discover the history of European art and appreciate the abilities of renowned painters over the centuries. The museum's quiet and well-maintained halls provide a wonderful backdrop for art fans and history buffs alike.

Location: The Fesch Museum is strategically positioned in the centre of Ajaccio, making it easily accessible to travelers touring the city. Its central position allows tourists to combine a visit to the museum with other surrounding sites, like the Ajaccio Cathedral, Maison Bonaparte, and the old town's picturesque streets.

In conclusion, the Fesch Museum in Ajaccio is a cultural jewel that highlights the artistic past of Europe. Its outstanding collection, together with its historical significance and stunning architectural setting, makes it a must-visit site for people interested in art, history, and Corsica's relationship to the greater European cultural environment.

Sanguinaires Islands Sunset

The Sanguinaires Islands Sunset, also known as "Les Îles Sanguinaires Sunset," is a beautiful natural beauty that brings people to the western coast of Corsica, France. These rocky islands, formally dubbed the "Isles of Blood," are famed for the breathtaking sunsets they produce, making them a favorite destination for visitors and photographers alike. Here's what you should expect when seeing the Sanguinaires Islands Sunset:

1. Dramatic Setting: The Sanguinaires Islands are located in the Mediterranean Sea, just a short distance from the town of Ajaccio in Corsica. The islands themselves, with their jagged, red granite formations, give a striking background to the sunset. The contrast between the black rocks and the blazing colours of the setting sun produces a compelling visual spectacle.

2. brilliant hues: As the sun begins to dip below the horizon, the sky over the Sanguinaires Islands is painted with a brilliant pallet of hues. Deep oranges, flaming reds, and delicate purples mingle together, providing a warm and ethereal glow over the islands and the water. The reflection of these colours on the calm Mediterranean waves adds to the charm.

3. Tranquil ambiance: The islands offer a quiet and tranquil ambiance, making it a great spot to unwind and savor the

natural beauty of the moment. The quiet ambience, along with the soothing sound of the waves, produces a sensation of serenity and relaxation.

4. Prime Viewing Locations: While the Sanguinaires Islands itself are a fantastic spot to observe the sunset, there are other prime viewing locations on the Corsican mainland, including stunning viewpoints and coastline walks. These vantage spots give clear views of the islands and the setting sun, allowing you to snap the ideal shot or simply absorb the moment.

5. Photographer's Paradise: The Sanguinaires Islands Sunset is a dream come true for photographers. The play of light and shadow, the brilliant hues, and the distinctive coastal terrain give countless opportunity for taking great images. Whether you're a professional or an amateur, this natural spectacle is likely to inspire your imagination.

6. wonderful Evening Activity: Visiting the Sanguinaires Islands for the sunset is a wonderful evening activity in Corsica. After a day of visiting the island, you may rest, absorb in the beauty, and watch as the sun drops below the horizon. Many travelers and residents assemble at the finest viewing sites to experience this memorable event.

7. Year-Round Attraction: While Corsica's Mediterranean environment ensures that sunsets may be experienced throughout the year, the summer months, from June to September, are particularly popular for watching the

Sanguinaires Islands Sunset owing to the continuously clear sky and pleasant temperatures.

In conclusion, the Sanguinaires Islands Sunset is a natural wonder that encapsulates the essence of Corsica's beauty. Whether you're looking a romantic evening, a tranquil moment of meditation, or the ideal image, this dazzling display of colors and light over the craggy islands is a must-experience sight for anybody visiting Corsica.

CHAPTER 2: LOCAL CUISINE

Corsican Delicacies

Corsican cuisine is a reflection of the island's distinct culture and nature. With a blend of Mediterranean and French influences, it features a choice of delectable and unusual meals. Here are some Corsican delicacies and specialties to excite your taste buds:

1. Brocciu: Brocciu is Corsica's most renowned cheese, a fresh and crumbly white cheese produced from sheep or goat's milk. It's a versatile element used in numerous Corsican cuisines, such as cannelloni and fiadone (a form of cheesecake). Brocciu's gentle and slightly acidic taste is a real Corsican treat.

2. Charcuterie: Corsican charcuterie is recognized across France. The island's rugged geography and vast meadows give great circumstances for rearing pigs. Sample delectable cured meats including coppa (air-dried pig neck), lonzu (pork loin), and figatellu (liver sausage). These meats are typically seasoned with local herbs and spices, delivering a blast of flavor.

3. Figatellu: Figatellu is a popular Corsican sausage prepared from ground pig and liver, seasoned with fragrant herbs and spices. It's often served grilled and combines nicely with a crusty bread.

4. Wild Game: Corsica's natural landscapes are home to wild boar and game birds, making game dishes a popular choice. Try meals like civet de sanglier (wild boar stew) or turtelli (pigeon pie) for a taste of Corsican hunting traditions.

5. fish: Given Corsica's seaside position, delicious fish abounds. Savor grilled fish, seafood stews, and bouillabaisse-inspired foods. The island's seafood is known for its quality and taste.

6. Corsican Wines: Corsica is a wine-producing region with a long history. Look for wines created from native grape varietals including Nielluccio and Sciaccarello for reds, and Vermentino for whites. These wines frequently have distinctive, terroir-driven qualities.

7. Canistrelli: Canistrelli are Corsican biscuits, sometimes comparable to biscotti. They come in numerous tastes, including anise and almond. These crispy nibbles are excellent for dipping in coffee or enjoying as a sweet snack.

8. Castagnaccio: Corsica's chestnut trees have given food for ages. Castagnaccio is a dessert prepared with chestnut flour, water, and olive oil, scented with rosemary and sometimes raisins or nuts. It's a rustic and earthy pleasure.

9. Corsican Honey: Corsican honey is widely renowned for its quality and unusual tastes. The island's unique

vegetation, including maquis plants and chestnut blooms, adds to the particular taste of Corsican honey.

10. Fiadone: Fiadone is a Corsican cheesecake prepared with brocciu cheese, eggs, sugar, and lemon zest. It's a simple yet wonderful dish that displays the creamy, slightly tangy brocciu.

11. Corsican plants & Spices: The maquis, Corsica's fragrant scrubland, is replete with aromatic plants including rosemary, thyme, and oregano. These herbs are used to flavor many Corsican foods, imparting a delicious depth of taste.

12. Acquavita: Wrap off your Corsican dinner with a sip of acquavita, a native grappa-like liquor sometimes mixed with herbs or fruits. It's a bold but fragrant way to complete your gastronomic voyage.

Corsican cuisine is a celebration of local products and traditional flavors, making it a must-explore component of your stay to this lovely Mediterranean island. Whether you're dining in local restaurants, visiting markets, or having a picnic with Corsican specialties, you're in for a gourmet trip filled with unique and savory pleasures.

Must-Try Restaurants

Corsica is recognized for its rich and diverse food, and there are many excellent restaurants around the island where you may sample real Corsican specialties. Here are several must-try restaurants in Corsica, offering a range of gastronomic experiences:

1. Le Don Quichotte (Bonifacio): This restaurant, located in the lovely village of Bonifacio, is famed for its fresh fish dishes. Enjoy a dinner on the patio overlooking the magnificent cliffs and the Mediterranean Sea. Don't miss the grilled fish and seafood platters.

2. L'Auberge du Prunelli (Ajaccio): For a taste of Corsican tastes in Ajaccio, visit L'Auberge du Prunelli. This intimate restaurant provides typical Corsican delicacies, including charcuterie, brocciu-based meals, and savory stews.

3. A Nepita (Calvi): A Nepita is a delightful restaurant in Calvi noted for its innovative Corsican cuisine. The menu contains a combination of traditional and contemporary foods, making it a fantastic spot to discover the island's culinary heritage with a modern touch.

4. Chez Seraphin (Corte): Located in the center of Corte, Chez Seraphin is a popular destination for traditional Corsican food. Try their wild boar delicacies, fresh cheeses, and substantial mountain cuisine. The intimate atmosphere contributes to the whole eating experience.

5. Le 20123 (Zonza): Le 20123 in Zonza is set in the picturesque Alta Rocca area of Corsica. It offers a farm-to-table eating experience with an emphasis on locally produced products. Their creative menu reflects the finest of Corsican products.

6. L'Antica (Bastia): L'Antica in Bastia is famed for its seafood, with dishes like lobster spaghetti and grilled fish taking center stage. The restaurant's position near the historic harbor adds to its attractiveness.

7. La Lucciola (Propriano): Situated in the seaside village of Propriano, La Lucciola provides spectacular sea views and a menu incorporating Corsican and Mediterranean cuisine. Their seafood and pasta dishes are particularly popular.

8. U Santa Marina (Porto-Vecchio): U Santa Marina, in Porto-Vecchio, is a Michelin-starred restaurant famed for its gourmet Corsican meals. The chef cleverly blends local ingredients to produce unforgettable eating experiences.

9. Le Monte Cinto (Corte): For a taste of Corsican mountain cuisine, travel to Le Monte Cinto in Corte. This restaurant focuses in robust, traditional meals like civet de sanglier (wild boar stew) and chestnut-based delicacies.

10. Le Casadelmar (Porto-Vecchio): Le Casadelmar is a Michelin-starred restaurant located in Porto-Vecchio. It offers a great dining experience with a focus on Mediterranean and Corsican tastes. The restaurant's

exquisite location and superb service make it a memorable choice for a special occasion.

Remember to make reservations, especially during the high tourist season, since these famous eateries might get fully booked quickly. Whether you're in Corsica to explore the beach, the mountains, or the ancient cities, these restaurants provide a wonderful opportunity to immerse yourself in the island's rich culinary traditions.

Ajaccio's Best Cafe's

Ajaccio, the capital city of Corsica, has a beautiful café culture where you can relax, enjoy the Mediterranean ambiance, and savor great coffee and pastries. Here are some of the top cafés in Ajaccio where you may enjoy in a great coffee break:

1. Café de la Place: Located in the heart of Ajaccio's ancient town, Café de la Place is a traditional choice for coffee enthusiasts. It offers a perfect spot for people-watching while you enjoy your coffee on the outside patio. Their pastries and croissants are also highly acclaimed.

2. Le Bistrot des Lices: Le Bistrot des Lices is a beautiful café near Place Foch. It's noted for its friendly and welcoming atmosphere. Enjoy a broad assortment of coffee beverages, including espresso and cappuccino, while appreciating the view of the neighboring Napoleon Bonaparte statue.

3. Café Napoléon: As the name implies, Café Napoléon pays homage to Corsica's most renowned historical figure. This cafe offers a comfortable and classy ambience. Besides superb coffee, you may indulge in Corsican delicacies like canistrelli biscuits and brocciu cheesecake.

4. Le Bistrot des Quais: Le Bistrot des Quais is a waterfront bistro located along the Quai des Martyrs. Enjoy your coffee

with a lovely view of the Ajaccio port. It's a fantastic setting for a leisurely breakfast or a relaxed afternoon break.

5. Le Gloria: Le Gloria is a popular cafe located on the Cours Napoléon, Ajaccio's main thoroughfare. It's noted for its speciality coffees and a range of teas. The elegant interior and outdoor dining make it a popular place for residents and visitors alike.

6. Café Nautique: Café Nautique offers a unique experience directly on the Ajaccio beach. It's a beachside cafe where you may sip your coffee with your toes on the sand. The laid-back ambience and ocean views make it a perfect choice for a quiet coffee break.

7. Le Petit Café: Le Petit Café is a charming and rustic cafe nestled away in Ajaccio's old town. It's noted for its warm service and a menu that offers a range of coffee selections. The ambience feels like a quaint Corsican house.

8. Le Lounge Café: For those wanting a more modern and trendy café experience, Le Lounge Café is a fashionable alternative. It provides a range of coffee drinks, beverages, and light nibbles. The modern decor and music make a dynamic atmosphere.

9. Le 1811 Café: Le 1811 Café, located near the Ajaccio Cathedral, provides a combination of Corsican and Italian cuisine. Enjoy coffee and pastries in a tranquil and historic atmosphere.

10. Le Napoléon Café: Le Napoléon Café is another cafe with a historical motif dedicated to Napoleon Bonaparte. It's a nice location to unwind with a cup of coffee and perhaps a slice of Corsican cheesecake.

When in Ajaccio, taking the time to visit these cafés not only enables you appreciate outstanding coffee but also allows you to drink in the city's lovely ambience and Corsican culture. Whether you like a classic café or a more contemporary atmosphere, there's a coffee shop in Ajaccio to fit your interests and preferences.

CHAPTER 3: ACTIVITIES

Beaches and Watersports

Beaches

Corsica, with its unique coastline and pure waters, is home to some of the most magnificent beaches in the Mediterranean. Whether you desire serenity, water activities, or picturesque vistas, Corsica offers a beach to fit your interests. Here are some of the top beaches on the island:

1. Palombaggia Beach (Porto-Vecchio): This renowned beach is noted for its beautiful white sand and crystal-clear blue seas. Palombaggia is great for sunbathing, swimming, and snorkeling. There are also coastal restaurants where you may sample Corsican cuisine.

2. Santa Giulia Beach (Porto-Vecchio): Santa Giulia is another famous beach in Porto-Vecchio, famed for its shallow, quiet waves. It's perfect for families and provides activities like paddleboarding and kayaking.

3. Rondinara Beach (Bonifacio): Rondinara is generally recognized as one of Corsica's most beautiful beaches, owing to its crescent shape and peaceful waves. It's a fantastic area for swimming and relaxing.

4. Loto Beach (Piana): Located in the Gulf of Porto, Loto Beach is famed for its red rock formations and stunning backdrop. The pristine waters are great for swimming and snorkeling.

5. Saleccia Beach (St-Florent): Accessible by boat or a tough climb, Saleccia Beach is an isolated paradise with white sands and blue waves. It's a nice area for leisure and picnics.

6. Ostriconi Beach (L'Île-Rousse): Ostriconi Beach offers a more natural environment, surrounded by dunes. It's a terrific alternative for those wanting a calmer beach experience.

7. Lotu Beach (St-Florent): Located near Saleccia Beach, Lotu Beach is accessible by boat and offers a calm and picturesque atmosphere. You may hire kayaks or paddleboards to enjoy the pristine seas.

8. Pinarello Beach (Sainte-Lucie-de-Porto-Vecchio): Pinarello Beach features a wonderful harbor with calm seas. It's popular for water activities including windsurfing and jet-skiing.

9. Calvi Beach (Calvi): Calvi Beach, in the lovely town of Calvi, provides a lengthy stretch of sand and gorgeous waves. It's wonderful for sunbathing and swimming, with a backdrop of the town's old fortress.

10. Algajola Beach (Algajola): Algajola Beach blends sandy shoreline with a lovely ancient town background. It's perfect for swimming, and there are watersports facilities available.

11. Tamarone Beach (Cap Corse): Located in Cap Corse, Tamarone Beach is a pebble beach with a rocky, untamed vibe. It's less congested than some of the more popular beaches, making it excellent for people seeking quiet.

12. Malfalcu Beach (Bonifacio): Malfalcu Beach is concealed among the rocks of Bonifacio. Accessible by boat or a hard climb, it's a quiet hideaway with crystal-clear waters.

13. Ghjunchitu Beach (Desert des Agriates): This secluded beach is accessible by boat or a spectacular stroll across the Desert des Agriates. It's a hidden paradise with white sands and tranquil waves.

Corsica's beaches appeal to a broad range of interests, from family-friendly locations to secluded, hidden gems. Whether you're wanting to relax, investigate undersea life, or enjoy water sports, Corsica's beaches offer a magnificent background for your Mediterranean trip.

Watersports

Ajaccio, Corsica's main city, is a lovely seaside location with a plethora of water sports activities. Ajaccio, located on the western coast of this magnificent Mediterranean island, with crystal-clear waters, a temperate climate, and a broad choice of water sports activities to suit all interests and ability levels. Ajaccio has something for everyone, whether you're a seasoned water sports enthusiast or a newbie eager to try something new.

1. Sailing & Yachting: Ajaccio's strategic location on the Gulf of Ajaccio makes it an outstanding sailing and yachting destination. The protected harbour offers ideal sailing conditions for both novice and expert sailors. You may rent a sailboat or a yacht to explore the Corsican coastline, visit adjacent islands, or simply cruise along the shore.

2. Windsurfing and Kitesurfing: The strong and constant winds that blow over the Gulf of Ajaccio make windsurfing and kitesurfing ideal. Beginners may learn to ride at local schools, while experienced riders can sail out to sea and catch the wind for a thrilling ride. Shallow waters along the beach are good for novices, while the wide sea provides more difficult conditions for skilled riders.

3. Stand-Up Paddleboarding (SUP): SUP is a great method to explore Ajaccio's coastline and its amazing marine life. Rent a paddleboard and float down the shoreline casually, or explore further out into the Gulf for a more strenuous

exercise. SUP is also an excellent opportunity to admire Ajaccio's rocky cliffs and secret bays.

4. Scuba Diving and Snorkeling: The undersea environment near Ajaccio is a diver's and snorkeler's paradise. This is a must-see location for underwater aficionados due to its crystal-clear waters, teeming marine life, and various diving opportunities. Explore coral reefs, underwater caverns, and historic shipwrecks while learning about the Mediterranean Sea's rich biodiversity.

5. Jet Skiing: Jet skiing is a popular option for individuals looking for an adrenaline rush. Rent jet skis and race over the Gulf of Ajaccio, experiencing the thrill of speed and the breathtaking coastline vistas. you guarantee a safe and pleasurable trip, make sure you follow local legislation and safety requirements.

6. Kayaking and Canoeing: Exploring the coastline of Ajaccio by kayak or canoe is a calm and environmentally beneficial way to connect with nature. Paddle through secret coves, explore sea caves, and enjoy the stunning surroundings at your own speed. Rentals and guided excursions are offered for people of all skill levels.

7. Fishing: Ajaccio has superb fishing prospects. There are lots of choices for beach fishing, deep sea fishing, and fly fishing in the island's rivers. The area is well-known for its rich marine life, which includes sea bream, sea bass, and amberjack.

8. Parasailing: This activity offers a unique perspective of Ajaccio's coastline. Soar far above the ocean while tied to a parachute, providing amazing views of the city, sea, and surrounding environment.

9. Boat Tours: If you want to explore the seas of Ajaccio in a more casual manner, try taking a boat trip. There are several alternatives available, ranging from short excursions around the harbor to day trips to surrounding islands such as the Îles Sanguinaires (Bloody Islands), which are famed for their spectacular red rock formations.

To summarize, Ajaccio is a water sports paradise for people of all interests and ability levels. This quaint Corsican city has it everything, whether you're looking for adrenaline-pumping thrills or peaceful moments of leisure by the ocean. Ajaccio is a great location for anybody wishing to enjoy the excitement of water activities while surrounded by spectacular surroundings, thanks to its stunning natural beauty, abundant marine life, and mild Mediterranean climate. Pack your swimwear, sunscreen, and spirit of adventure, and prepare to create some wonderful experiences on the waves of Ajaccio.

Hiking Trails

Corsica, particularly the region surrounding Ajaccio, is known for its breathtaking natural beauty and different terrain, making it a hiker's dream. There are hiking routes near Ajaccio to suit all levels of fitness and adventure, whether you're an experienced trekker or just want to enjoy a peaceful walk in nature. Here are some prominent hiking paths in the region to explore:

1. Sentier des Crêtes (walk of the Ridges): This difficult and rewarding walk provides panoramic views of the Gulf of Ajaccio, the Sanguinaires Islands, and the surrounding mountains. It's a challenging trek with steep ascents and descents through Corsican scrubland and rocky terrain. The path runs from the Calanques de Piana to the Col de Verghio, traversing through some of Corsica's most stunning scenery.

2. Mare e Monti: This long-distance hiking trail provides a variety of sceneries, from coastal trails with sea vistas to highland territory. It is separated into two halves, the northern beginning in Calenzana and the southern beginning in Porto. Both portions provide numerous possibilities to learn about Corsica's flora and animals, visit picturesque villages, and swim in the Mediterranean's crystal-clear waters.

3. Capo di Feno Loop: The Capo di Feno loop route is a shorter and more accessible option that leads you to the Capo di Feno peninsula, immediately west of Ajaccio. This round path provides panoramic views of the Gulf of Ajaccio and its surroundings. It's ideal for a half-day walk or a leisurely stroll among the maquis.

4. Cascade des Anglais (English Waterfall): Located in the Prunelli Gorges, this climb leads to a beautiful waterfall known as the Cascade des Anglais. Because the track is reasonably straightforward, it is ideal for families and people seeking a less rigorous trek. It's an opportunity to take in the gorgeous Corsican landscape while cooling yourself in the cold waters of the waterfall.

5. Monte Gozzi: For a one-of-a-kind trekking adventure, attempt Monte Gozzi, a spectacular rocky peak visible from Ajaccio. The fairly difficult trek provides panoramic views of the Gulf of Ajaccio, the Sanguinaires Islands, and the surrounding countryside. It's especially beautiful during sunrise and sunset.

6. Sentier des Douaniers (Customs Officers' Path): This seaside path near Porto-Pollo provides breathtaking views of the Mediterranean Sea. It's a short stroll that allows you to discover secret coves, swim in isolated beaches, and admire the beauty of Corsica's coastline.

7. Les Îles Sanguinaires (The Bloody Islands): While not a standard hiking track, seeing the Îles Sanguinaires by boat

is a must for nature lovers. These islands are famous for their distinctive red rock formations and abundance of wildlife. You may walk around the main island, Isola di Mezzu Mare, discovering its lighthouse and natural beauty.

Before beginning on any hiking expedition in the Ajaccio region, verify local trail conditions, collect maps or GPS coordinates, and ensure you have the necessary equipment and supplies. Corsica's terrain may be challenging, so careful planning is essential. The hiking paths surrounding Ajaccio give an opportunity to immerse yourself in the island's spectacular natural landscapes and create lasting memories of your stay, whether you're searching for a demanding multi-day excursion or a casual nature walk.

Boat Tours

The capital of Corsica, Ajaccio, is not only a city with a rich historical past but also a starting point for seeing some of the most breathtaking coastal vistas in the Mediterranean. Taking a boat excursion is one of the greatest ways to experience this French island's splendor to the fullest. These Ajaccio boat cruises provide visitors the chance to discover isolated coves, spotless beaches, and undiscovered treasures along the untamed Corsican coastline. The experiences, locations, and advantages that boat trips in Ajaccio provide for tourists will be highlighted in this article.

1. Wide Range of Tours

Ajaccio offers a variety of boat cruises to suit a variety of tastes. There is a choice for you whether you want a relaxing cruise, an exhilarating adventure, or a romantic sunset sail. Popular boat cruises include the following:

Island Cruises: You may go swimming, snorkeling, and exploring secluded coves on these full-day or half-day excursions to surrounding islands including the Sanguinaires Islands.

Explore the stunning rocky inlets and cliffs of Corsica's calanques, which are frequently only accessible by boat.

Sunset & evening cruises: Spend a romantic evening on the water while sipping on Corsican wines and watching the sun set.

Several boat cruises provide possibilities for underwater exploration of Corsica's abundant marine life. Corsica is a diver's paradise.

2. Natural Wonders

The boat cruises offered in Ajaccio offer some of the most breathtaking natural beauty in the Mediterranean. The picture-perfect environment includes a rocky coastline, towering cliffs, clean waters, and immaculate beaches. Among the famous landmarks are:

The UNESCO-listed red granite rock formations known as Les Calanques de Piana are a popular stop on boat cruises. A photographer's paradise, they have distinct shapes and hues.

The Sanguinaires Islands are an archipelago that can be reached by boat from Ajaccio and are well-known for their vibrant marine life and beautiful red rock formations.

The Gulf of Porto is a protected area with a wide variety of plants and animals. Boat cruises here frequently stop at quaint fishing communities like Girolata.

3. Local knowledge

The expertise of seasoned captains and guides who lead boat tours in Ajaccio is one of the benefits. They can impart knowledge about the history, geology, and marine life of the area, making the excursion both aesthetically pleasing and intellectually stimulating.

4. Exciting Possibilities

The following are some thrilling experiences that Ajaccio boat cruises can provide for more daring tourists:

Watersports: Some trips provide kayaks, paddleboards, or even jet skis so that you may actively explore the coast.

Exploring caves: The coastline of Ajaccio is home to a number of sea caverns, and certain trips give visitors the chance to explore these amazing natural formations.

5. Leisure and Relaxation

Boat cruises, on the other hand, give visitors the chance to unwind and enjoy themselves. On the deck, you can take a sunbath, have a picnic in the Mediterranean, or just relax while sailing across the calm waters.

6. Conscientious travel

Responsible tourism is a priority for many boat excursion providers in Ajaccio. They place a high priority on preserving the delicate coastal habitat of Corsica and adhere to regulations to ensure little environmental effect.

7. Useful Advice

Booking in Advance: It's recommended to book your boat excursion in advance during the busiest travel season because popular tours can fill up quickly.

Weather considerations: Pay attention to the weather because choppy waters can affect the schedule and accessibility of tours.

What to Bring: Bring necessary items like sunscreen, a hat, sunglasses, and swimsuit depending on the type of tour you are taking.

Finally, boat cruises in Ajaccio provide a unique approach to discover the captivating coastal beauty of Corsica. These trips provide something for everyone, whether you're looking for adventure, relaxation, or an educational experience. These boat tours are a must-do when visiting Ajaccio because of the knowledge of the local guides, the captivating scenery, and the chance to find hidden jewels. They will leave you with memories to treasure for a lifetime.

Ajaccio's Vibrant Nightlife

The lovely seaside city of Ajaccio, which is located on the island of Corsica, comes alive when darkness falls over it. While Ajaccio is well known for its fascinating historical monuments, gorgeous beaches, and unspoiled landscape, it also has a lively nightlife culture that welcomes both locals and visitors. We'll examine in more detail what makes Ajaccio's nightlife so alluring in this piece, including the wide variety of bars and clubs, cultural events, and late-night dining alternatives.

1. Restaurants and bars along the beach

The Mediterranean Sea's proximity to Ajaccio offers a distinctive environment for beachside bars and restaurants that come alive at night. Imagine sipping cocktails while relaxing to the sound of the waves with your toes in the beach. A relaxed yet energetic environment is created by the live music played at some coastal restaurants.

2. Wine tasting in Corsica

It can be the highlight of your evening to partake in a wine tasting in Ajaccio because Corsica is known for producing top-notch wines. You can sample Corsican wines in many wine bars and cellars in the city and experience the flavors of this lovely island.

3. Dance floors and nightclubs

Ajaccio features a number of nightclubs and dance locations for people looking for a livelier nightlife experience. Local and foreign DJs frequently spin a variety of dance, pop, and electronic music in these establishments. Ajaccio's nightlife often begins around midnight, when clubs begin to fill up and the party lasts until early morning.

4. Festive Activities

Ajaccio has numerous festivals and events all year long that add to its thriving nightlife. These occasions, which range from music festivals to cultural celebrations, frequently feature live shows, outdoor markets, and street parties that keep the city's streets busy well into the night.

5. Live Performances and Music

The live music scene in Ajaccio will appeal to music lovers. Numerous restaurants and venues feature local bands and musicians, giving visitors the chance to personally experience Corsican musical traditions. There are performances of jazz, corsican traditional music, and even rock on various evenings of the week.

6. Late-Nite Restaurants

Lack of late-night dining options makes it impossible to have a thriving nightlife. In this respect, Ajaccio delivers. Up until the wee hours of the morning, you can discover a wide selection of eateries and food stands providing both Corsican delicacies and other types of cuisine.

7. Waterfront Walks

Consider taking a leisurely stroll around Ajaccio's waterfront promenade if you'd want a more laid-back evening. It's the perfect location for a calm evening with loved ones because of the lit-up coastline and the sight of boats softly bobbing in the harbor.

8. Accessibility and safety

The city of Ajaccio takes precautions to safeguard the safety of its citizens and visitors, and the city's nightlife is generally safe. Many nightlife venues are located in centralized areas, making it simple to walk between them and reducing the need for transportation.

9. Clothes Code

Even if some places have a more relaxed dress code, others might, especially if you intend to visit upscale bars or clubs. Checking the particular needs of the locations you wish to visit is a smart idea.

Conclusion: Whether you prefer dancing the night away, taking in live music, sampling local wines, or simply admiring the majesty of the Mediterranean at night, Ajaccio's dynamic nightlife offers a wide selection of experiences for all types of revelers. Because of the city's distinctive fusion of cultural traditions, breathtaking natural settings, and exciting entertainment opportunities, the enjoyment never ends there. Ajaccio unequivocally demonstrates that Corsica's allure endures into the wee hours, providing visitors with an amazing nightlife experience.

CHAPTER 4: DAY TRIPS

Scenic Drive to Calanques de Piana

The beautiful trip to the Calanques de Piana in Corsica, France, is a spectacular trek through some of the Mediterranean's most stunning scenery. This UNESCO World Heritage site is well-known for its distinctive red granite rock formations and crystal-clear rivers. Here's a rundown of the route and what to anticipate on this scenic drive:

Ajaccio is the starting point.

The voyage to the Calanques de Piana usually begins at Ajaccio, Corsica's capital. Ajaccio is famed for its historical significance, but it is also a gateway to the natural treasures of Corsica.

Route D81: The Scenic Highway From Ajaccio, follow Route D81, often known as the D81 Marine, which travels along Corsica's western coast. This route is famous for its breathtaking views of the Mediterranean Sea, steep cliffs, and lush maquis (Mediterranean scrubland). Keep the following highlights in mind as you go on this picturesque drive:

1. Gulf of Ajaccio: The drive opens with views of the Gulf of Ajaccio, which provides a beautiful introduction to the coastal splendor of Corsica.

2. Piana Calanches Signage: Look for signs directing you to the Calanches de Piana. Along the trip, you'll catch glimpses of the red granite rock formations.

3. Capo Rosso: On your way to the Calanches, you'll travel via Capo Rosso, a dramatic promontory with its own set of magnificent cliffs and geological structures. It's worth stopping here for more photo chances.

4. Arrival at the Calanques: The view becomes more stunning as you approach the Calanques de Piana. The route passes through tight, rugged terrain, providing vistas of the red cliffs and turquoise ocean below.

5. Parking and Exploration: There are parking spots available once you get to the Calanques de Piana. You may then explore the region on foot. The place is famous for its maze of small walkways and trails that wind among the rock formations, providing unique views of this natural wonder.

6. Sunset: If feasible, plan your visit to the Calanques de Piana around the sunset. The setting sun's golden colours on the red rocks create a very stunning ambiance.

7. Safety Reminder: While the trip is stunning, it is critical to drive carefully on the undulating and occasionally narrow roads. Drive gently and cautiously around other vehicles.

Return Trip: Once you've had your fill of the Calanques de Piana, you may take the same road back to Ajaccio, taking in the breathtaking scenery once more.

This gorgeous trip to the Calanques de Piana is more than simply a travel; it's an experience that connects you with Corsica's natural splendor. The red cliffs against the azure Mediterranean, along with the scented maquis, provide a sensory-rich journey you won't soon forget. Keep your camera handy since every curve in the road exposes another postcard-worthy beauty.

Visit to Bonifacio

A trip to Bonifacio is a trip to one of the most beautiful and historically significant places in Corsica, France. Bonifacio is a lovely and scenic town perched above spectacular limestone cliffs and overlooking the glittering Mediterranean Sea. It encourages visitors to enjoy its natural beauty, historical treasures, and dynamic culture. Here's a tip to making the most of your trip to Bonifacio:

1. Old Town and the Citadel: Begin your journey of Bonifacio at the town's core, the ancient Old Town. The streets are dotted with charming stores, restaurants, and cafés. Explore the Citadel, a stronghold dating from the 9th century. Views of the cliffs, harbor, and adjacent islands may be had from its ramparts.

2. The King of Aragon's Staircase: Descend the legendary King of Aragon's Staircase, a steep and twisting stone stairs that leads down to the sea. It's an astonishing technical marvel that allows access to marine caves and swimming holes.

3. Excursions & Boat Tours: Experience the gorgeous coastline by taking a boat cruise from the Bonifacio harbor. These tours frequently include visits to sea caves, secret coves, and excursions to surrounding islands such as the Lavezzi Islands, which are noted for their crystal-clear waters and marine life.

4. Marina Bonifacio: Stroll around the bustling marina, which is home to beautiful yachts and attractive waterfront eateries. It's a nice spot to eat or simply relax and enjoy the marine environment.

5. Beaches in Bonifacio: Relax at one of the neighboring beaches, such as Plage de la Tonnara or Plage de Sutta Rocca. White sand and blue waves characterize the beaches here.

6. Lighthouse of Bonifacio: PRACTICAL Views of the town, cliffs, and sea may be had from the Bonifacio Lighthouse. It's really beautiful at sunset.

7. Dining and Culinary Arts: Local eateries provide Corsican cuisine. Don't pass up the chance to sample traditional foods such as Corsican charcuterie, shellfish, and local wines.

8. The Grotto of Napoleon: Discover Napoleon's Grotto, a cave where the French emperor is said to have sought sanctuary during his exile. It's a fascinating historical location.

9. Festivals & Events: Check to see if any local events or festivals are taking place during your stay. Corsicans are noted for their boisterous festivities that frequently involve music, dance, and traditional acts.

10. Nature and hiking: - For nature lovers, Bonifacio has a number of hiking paths that take you into the beautiful Corsican countryside and provide spectacular views of the cliffs and coastline.

11. Practical Tips: During the peak summer months, Bonifacio may get busy, so plan your visit appropriately.

- When touring the Old Town, wear comfortable shoes because the streets might be steep and uneven.

- Dress appropriately for the warm Mediterranean weather and remain hydrated, especially if you intend to trek or spend time in the sun.

A visit to Bonifacio promises to be an amazing experience, combining natural beauty, historical charm, and Corsican warmth. Bonifacio provides a unique and enriching vacation experience on the beautiful island of Corsica, whether you're touring the Old Town, traveling along the coastline, or eating local cuisine.

Wine Tasting in the Corsican Vineyards

Corsica, the ruggedly beautiful Mediterranean Sea island, is not only a shelter for natural treasures, but also a treasure trove of vineyards producing wines with distinct character and flavor. Visitors to Corsica are given to a one-of-a-kind experience as they embark on a trip across the island's vineyards, with each taste revealing a tale of terroir, history, and a profound connection to the land. A full study of what awaiting people seeking the pleasures of wine tasting in Corsican vineyards is provided here.

1. Various Grape Varieties: Corsica has a diverse range of grape varietals, both indigenous and imported. Local grapes including Niellucciu, Sciaccarellu, Vermentinu, and Biancu Gentile add to the island's distinctive and diversified wine offerings.

2. Terroir Inflection: Corsican terroir, distinguished by its different microclimates and rough landscapes, is crucial in developing the tastes of the wines. Vineyards are frequently positioned on hillsides, benefiting from the cooling sea breezes and sufficient sunlight, which imparts a particular flavor to the grapes.

3. Vineyard Locations: Corsica is separated into wine-producing areas, each with its own distinct identity. Notable regions include Patrimonio, which is recognized for

its red wines, Ajaccio, which is known for its strong reds and crisp whites, and Figari, which is noted for its reds made from the indigenous Sciaccarellu grape.

4. Wine Trails: Traveling along Corsica's authorized wine roads is a sensory experience. These paths travel across lovely countryside, passing through vineyards, olive groves, and charming villages. The Patrimonio Wine Route, for example, is famous for its old vineyards and breathtaking surroundings.

5. Wineries Run by Families: Many Corsican wineries are family-run, with generations of knowledge passed down through the generations. Visiting these estates is a personal and intimate experience, with the winemaker frequently directing tastings and discussing the complexities of their craft.

Tours of Wine Cellars: Wine lovers can learn about the winemaking process through guided tours of cellars and vineyards. These trips provide a behind-the-scenes glimpse at the art of winemaking in Corsica, from the careful harvesting of grapes to the fermenting and aging processes.

7. Distinctive Wine Styles: Corsican wines come in a variety of types, ranging from crisp and lemony whites to powerful and complex reds. Organic and biodynamic processes are frequently used by the island's winemakers, resulting in wines that represent the purity of the fruit and the character of the region.

8. Wine and Food Pairing: Corsican cuisine, with its emphasis on local and seasonal ingredients, complements the island's wines perfectly. Enjoy the perfect pairing of a Vermentinu with fresh fish or a powerful Niellucciu with traditional Corsican charcuterie.

9. Wine Festivals & Events: Plan your trip to coincide with one of Corsica's wine festivals or events. These events bring together local winemakers, artisans, and wine enthusiasts, resulting in a dynamic atmosphere packed with music, dancing, and, of course, plenty of wine tasting.

10. Environmentally Friendly Practices: - Many Corsican winemakers are committed to environmentally friendly procedures and conserving the island's natural beauty. This dedication provides a new level of appreciation for the wines produced in this exceptional terroir.

11. Tasting Experiences to Remember: - Whether you visit a contemporary vineyard with cutting-edge technology or a rustic, centuries-old estate, each wine tasting in Corsica is an exploration of the island's winemaking legacy.

12. Practical Considerations: - It is best to schedule tastings ahead of time, especially during peak tourist seasons.

- Consider hiring a local guide to help you explore the wine trails and learn about the history and culture of Corsican winemaking.

- Don't miss out on wine bars and restaurants that highlight the variety of Corsican wines by offering by-the-glass alternatives and skillfully crafted lists.

Finally, wine tasting in Corsican vineyards is a sensory experience that extends beyond the taste. It's a journey through landscapes molded by centuries of viticulture, a celebration of rare grape varietals, and a meeting with passionate winemakers who value tradition while welcoming innovation. Visitors to Corsica find a piece of the island's soul with each glass, making wine tasting an essential component of the Corsican travel narrative. Cheers to the enchantment of Corsican wines and the stories they tell.

CHAPTER 5: SHOPPING

Ajaccio's Markets

The capital of Corsica, Ajaccio, is tucked away along the lovely Mediterranean shores and is not only a city rich in history but also a thriving center for gastronomic treats. Corsica's markets, which are brimming with produce from the land and the sea, are evidence of its long agricultural and nautical history. We will stroll around the stalls, sample the flavors, and delve into the cultural tapestry that defines this alluring city in our study of Ajaccio's marketplaces.

The Central Market in Ajaccio (Le Marché Central): Locals and visitors alike are attracted into a kaleidoscope of colors and fragrances at Ajaccio's Central Market, which has been dubbed "A Symphony of Colors and fragrances." This thriving market is located in the city's center, close to Place Foch, and is a veritable treasure trove of seasonal food, regional delicacies, and handcrafted goods.

Fresh Foods Abound: Explore the stalls filled with colorful produce and herbs that came straight from Corsican farms. Offerings in the market change with the seasons, showcasing the island's diverse agricultural production.

Delights of Corsican Charcuterie and Cheese: The Central Market in Ajaccio is a sanctuary for those who enjoy Corsican charcuterie and cheese. Enjoy coppa, lonzu, and other types of cured meats while learning about the delicate flavors of corsican cheeses like brocciu and casgiu merzu.

Given Ajaccio's coastal position, the market also offers a remarkable selection of seafood. Seafood lovers can enjoy the abundance of the ocean, which includes delicious shellfish and recently caught fish.

2. The Fish Market in Ajaccio (Le Marché aux Poissons):

Harbor Freshness: Ajaccio's Fish Market, which is close to the Central Market, is a bustling scene where the morning's catch takes center stage. Corsica's tight connection to the sea is shown by the local fishermen's exhibition of their bounty.

Catch of the Day: Wander around the kiosks filled with shining fish, squid, and shellfish and take in the seaside ambiance. The variety is as astonishing as it is fresh, ranging from traditional Mediterranean dishes like red mullet to Corsican delicacies like langoustines.

Seafood Gastronomy: The Fish Market offers a chance to learn about Corsican seafood gastronomy in addition to being a place to buy fish. Many of the kiosks provide prepared foods, enabling guests to enjoy the flavors of the Mediterranean directly on the waterfront.

Events and Specialty Markets: Marché des Producteurs de Pays: This sporadic market, held in several Ajaccio sites, features the finest Corsican handcrafted goods. It's a great chance to interact directly with regional producers of anything from cured meats and wines to honey and olive oil.

Ajaccio has festivals honoring Corsican cuisine, which frequently include speciality markets. By bringing together chefs, producers, and food lovers, these festivals foster a vibrant environment for gastronomic exploration.

4. Beyond Food: Souvenirs and Crafts Handcrafted Treasures: Ajaccio's markets provide more than just delectable foods. Learn about Corsican workmanship and culture as you peruse the stalls selling handmade items like crafts, jewelry, textiles, and souvenirs.

5. Advice for Market Research: Timing Is Crucial Plan your visit for the morning when the markets are bustling with fresh produce and the atmosphere is upbeat if you want to see them at their liveliest.

Engage the Community: Engage the vendors in discussion. Many of them are proud artisans who are eager to impart knowledge about their work and the Corsican way of life.

Bring a tummy for food Numerous vendors provide tastings. Expect to enjoy some of the best cheeses, charcuterie, and other delicacies that Corsica has to offer.

In conclusion, the markets in Ajaccio are more than just places to purchase; they are immersive encounters that provide a glimpse into Corsican culture. Every visit is a culinary adventure, an exploration of customs, and an opportunity to experience the genuine flavors of Ajaccio and Corsica as a whole, from the vivacious Central Market to the briny appeal of the Fish Market.

Unique Souvenirs

It's not simply the magnificent scenery and intriguing historical sites that stand out when visiting the charming city of Ajaccio in Corsica. A variety of one-of-a-kind souvenirs, each reflecting a different aspect of Corsican character, are abundant thanks to the dynamic local craftsmanship and culture. Ajaccio offers a wide variety of distinctive souvenirs to select from, whether you're looking for a memento of the island's fascinating history, a taste of its gastronomic delights, or a work of exquisite skill.

Charcuterie from Corsica: Corsican charcuterie is a type of culinary art, and bringing these tasty treats home is a gift for any food aficionado. Corsican charcuterie includes Coppa, Lonzu, and Figatellu. The dishes coppa, lonzu (cured pig loin), and figatellu (pork sausage) are a few examples of those that best represent Corsican cuisine. To make transporting simpler, look for vacuum-sealed packaging.

2. Cheese from Corsica: Brocciu and Casgiu Merzu: A specialty of Corsica is brocciu, a fresh cheese made from sheep or goat milk. It goes well with the pungent and robust Casgiu Merzu, a typical blue cheese from Corsica. These cheeses have a unique flavor and reflect the pastoral traditions of the island.

3. Wines from Corsica: Corsica makes distinct and tasty wines using the varietals vermentino and sciaccarellu. For whites, seek out wines made from the native Vermentino grape, and for reds, Sciaccarellu. Wine from Corsica is more than just a drink; it offers a taste of the island's terroir.

4. Olive oil from Corsica: Huile d'Olive Corse: Corsican olive oil is prized for its high quality and is derived from the island's historic olive groves. For foodies or those who enjoy the subtleties of good olive oil, it makes the ideal gift.

5. Honey from Corsica: Corsican honey is a delectable sweet and fragrant dessert. Corsican honey has distinct flavors because of the island's varied vegetation. To get a sense of Corsica's natural landscapes, look for honey variations like chestnut or maquis honey.

6. Herbal liqueurs from Corsica: Discover Corsica's herbal traditions by tasting liqueurs prepared from regional plants, like myrtle and chestnut. Both chestnut liqueur and myrtle liqueur, which both perfectly capture the flavor of Corsican terroir, are popular choices.

7. Corsican ceramics: Ceramic creations: Ajaccio is home to skilled craftspeople who create distinctive pottery. These hand-painted ceramics range from ornamental plates to classic Corsican pitchers known as "cassettes," and they are both lovely and useful.

8. Essential Oils from Corsica: Aromatic Extravagance: High-quality essential oils are made from aromatic plants native to Corsica, like immortelle and lavender. These oils not only convey island scents but also have a number of health advantages.

9. Fragrances from Corsica: Fragrances of the Maquis: Corsican perfume makers are inspired by the maquis on the island to create perfumes that perfectly encapsulate the Mediterranean. Look for colognes with myrtle, juniper, and wildflower scents.

10. Corsage (Pouch) from Corsica: Pouches: Local artists frequently create traditional Corsican corsages, little fabric pouches decorated with Corsican emblems. They make for adorable and useful keepsakes that are great for holding little things or acting as decorative pieces.

11. Handmade Soaps from Corsica: Fragrant Memories: Artisanal soaps from Corsica, frequently produced with regional components like olive oil and herbs, provide a sensual remembrance of the island. Several perfumes influenced by Corsican flora are available.

When choosing souvenirs in Ajaccio, think about perusing neighborhood markets and artisan stores to find special finds. The distinctive keepsakes of Ajaccio, whether they be a taste of Corsican cuisine, a drink of its wines, or a work of artisanal craftsmanship, are more than just trinkets; they are representations of Corsican identity and the recollections of an enthralling adventure.

Boutiques and Local Crafts

The Corsican capital of Ajaccio is a refuge for anyone looking for distinctive and genuine regional crafts in addition to being a city steeped in history and natural beauty. You may find businesses and studios that represent Corsica's artistic essence as you stroll through its lovely alleyways. Here is a guide to shopping in Ajaccio's shops and discovering the regional crafts, which range from handcrafted ceramics to traditional Corsican fabrics

1. La Maison du Cèdre, first: La Maison du Cèdre is a charming store where you can browse a variety of handcrafted fragrances and soaps that are inspired by the aromas of Corsica. Notes of cedar, myrtle, and other fragrant plants are frequently found in fragrances.

2. The Bougies' Workshop: L'Atelier des Bougies is a workshop in Corsica that specializes in creating excellent candles. These candles, which are frequently perfumed with Corsican scents, are both useful and beautiful keepsakes.

3. U Scontru (Pottery created by hand): U Scontru is a pottery studio where you can discover ceramics made by hand that showcase Corsican workmanship. These one-of-a-kind items, which range from colorful plates to useful utensils, encapsulate the spirit of the island.

4. Design by Corsica: Modern Corsican Designs: Corsica Design is a store that features modern designs that draw

inspiration from Corsican customs. You'll discover a carefully chosen selection of gifts, accessories, and home goods that combine native Corsican design with contemporary aesthetics.

5. The Campo del Monte Farm: La Ferme de Campo di Monte is more than just a store; it's a farm where you can get Corsican honey and other related goods. The farm's store sells a range of honey, candles made from beeswax, and other products associated with bees.

6. Corsica Occidentale: Traditional fabrics from Corsica: Corsica Nustrale is a store that specializes in fabrics from the region. The shop sells furnishings made from textiles decorated with Corsican motifs, such as tablecloths and pillows, to give your house a bit of the island.

7. Land of Light: Jewelry inspired by the culture and natural beauty of Corsica may be found in Terra di Lume, a jewelry store. These works of art, which range from bracelets with symbolic charms to necklaces embellished with maquis plants, each convey a tale of the island.

8. A Casarella is a quaint shop that sells a range of Corsican gifts, from handcrafted trinkets to locally produced jams and preserves. For those looking for a wide selection of real souvenirs, this is the place to go.

9. The Comtale Cave: La Cave Comtale, which sells Corsican wines and spirits, offers wine connoisseurs an experience

rather than merely a wine store. Discover a new favorite to take home by perusing a carefully picked collection of Corsican wines, liqueurs, and spirits.

10. The Bougie and Savon Workshop: The Candle and Soap Atelier is a workshop that specializes in making candles and soaps the old-fashioned way. You may see the handmade process in action and pick from a variety of exquisitely made goods.

11. The Piana Calanches, Items Made in Corsica: Les Calanches de Piana is a store where you can discover a variety of items made in Corsica, including olive oils, jams, and handicrafts. You may discover the variety of Corsican workmanship there.

Take the time to talk to the craftsmen as you explore these stores and workshops; many of them are eager to share the inspirations behind their products. The shops and regional crafts of Ajaccio, which invite you to bring home a piece of the island's artistic essence, give a glimpse into the artistic tapestry of Corsica, whether you're looking for a one-of-a-kind present or a personal souvenir.

CHAPTER 6: PRACTICAL INFORMATION

Accommodation Options

Ajaccio's lodging options: Corsican hospitality meets comfort

Selecting the ideal lodging as you prepare for your trip to Ajaccio, Corsica, is crucial for a relaxing and pleasurable stay. Accommodations in Ajaccio range from boutique hotels with a Mediterranean flair to beachfront resorts that showcase the island's natural beauty. Here is a resource to assist you in learning more about Ajaccio's lodging possibilities:

Old Town boutique hotels, for example:

1. Atmosphere: For a really Corsican experience, think about booking a stay in a boutique hotel tucked away in the city's famed Old Town of Ajaccio. These quaint lodgings frequently have stone walls, distinctive furnishings, and

attentive service. They offer the ideal fusion of contemporary comforts and a bygone era.

2. Resorts along the Sea: Ajaccio is home to a number of opulent beachfront resorts with breathtaking views of the Mediterranean Sea. These resorts frequently include large accommodations, luxurious facilities, and direct beach access. For those looking for a luxurious and peaceful getaway, it is the perfect option.

3. Apartments and vacation rentals: Home Away from Home: Apartments and vacation rentals provide you the freedom to explore Ajaccio as a native would. Whether you choose a villa with a sea view or a delightful apartment in the Old Town, this choice offers a more unique and tailored experience.

4. Hotels Near Waterfront: Panoramic Views: Hotels that border Ajaccio's waterfront provide breath-taking views of the port. By choosing lodging near the water, you may take in the splendor of the Mediterranean from your window or balcony. The majority of these hotels are close to the city's top sights via foot.

5. Hotels that welcome families: Comfort for All Ages: If you're traveling with children, seek for hotels that are kid-friendly and can accommodate both adults and kids. These hotels frequently provide roomy accommodations, kid-friendly features, and perhaps even planned activities for young visitors.

6. Budget-friendly Alternatives: Hostels & Low-Cost Hotels: For those who want to spend as much money as possible on discovery, Ajaccio also has low-cost lodging alternatives. Budget hotels and hostels provide basic facilities while letting you save money on lodging.

7. Inns and B&Bs: Warm Hospitality: Bed and breakfasts in Corsica, or "chambres d'hôtes," provide a welcoming and individualized experience. The warm welcome and local knowledge that hosts frequently provide their visitors helps to make their stay more personal.

8. Retreats for health: Rejuvenation & Relaxation: Ajaccio offers wellness resorts that pair Corsica's natural beauty with rejuvenation amenities including spas, yoga, and holistic therapies. For those looking for a restorative experience, these getaways are ideal.

9. Hotels for business: Business travelers seeking comfort can think about booking a room at one of Ajaccio's corporate hotels. These lodgings frequently provide conveniences including conference spaces, fast internet, and good locations.

10. Farmstays (Agriturismi): Explore the agriturismi in the countryside surrounding Ajaccio for a unique experience. These farm stays give you the chance to interact with Corsican rural life, sample local food, and take in the natural beauty of the island.

Camping and glam camping: Camping grounds and glamping choices are available for people who wish to get close to Corsica's unspoiled natural beauty. To take advantage of both metropolitan conveniences and the peace of nature, pick a location close to Ajaccio.

Think about the reason for your trip, your desired lodging option, and the features that are most important to you before making a reservation. Whether you're looking for an opulent getaway, a modest hideaway, or a family-friendly setting, Ajaccio has a wide selection of lodging choices to meet your preferences.

Transportation Tips

Ajaccio invites visitors to discover its charming streets and breathtaking scenery because of its compelling fusion of history, culture, and natural beauty. With a variety of transportation choices that meet a wide range of interests and needs, navigating this Corsican treasure is a breeze. These travel suggestions will guarantee a smooth and comfortable trip regardless of whether you choose to drive across Corsica's harsh landscape or explore the Old Town on foot.

1. Walking around the waterfront and in the Old Town: Ajaccio's Old Town, with its congested streets and important landmarks, is best explored on foot. Explore the quaint streets, find the secret squares, and stroll along the promenade beside the lake. Most of the city's top attractions, such the museums, marketplaces, and the birthplace of Napoleon, are conveniently close by. **2.

2. Biking in Ajaccio: Cycling Through the Scenery: To tour Ajaccio and its surrounds, think about hiring a bike. A leisurely method to explore the city's streets and seafront is by bicycle, which is also a sustainable form of transportation. There are numerous bike paths in Ajaccio.

3. Utilizing Public Transportation: Services for buses and trains: Ajaccio has a well-connected system of public

transportation that makes it simple to get throughout the city and to neighboring cities. Buses are an easy method to get between neighborhoods, but trains may take you farther away and provide beautiful scenery along the route.

4. Renting a car to explore an island Freedom to Roam: Take into account hiring a car to thoroughly explore Corsica's varied landscapes. This choice gives you the freedom to travel to places that could be difficult for you to get by public transit, such as the highlands, coastal highways, and hidden jewels. There are several car rental companies in Ajaccio that provide a selection of vehicles.

5. Scenic Drives Corsican Landscapes on Wheels: Ajaccio is a great place to start if you want to travel throughout the island of Corsica, which is known for its beautiful drives. Take a drive to the Calanques de Piana, the interior mountains, or any of the stunning beaches that along the coastline.

Boat excursions and ferries:

6. Island-Hopping Excursions: Due to its coastline location, Ajaccio serves as a hub for travel to other Corsican locations. With boat cruises and ferries, visit surrounding islands like the Lavezzi Islands. These tours provide you the chance to explore remote beaches, marine life, and the stunning Mediterranean scenery.

7. Taxi Services: Convenient Point-to-Point transport: Taxis can be a practical alternative for point-to-point transport because they are widely accessible in Ajaccio. Taxis offer a convenient and pleasant service, whether you require a trip from the airport, help with your luggage, or transportation to a specified area.

8. Airport shuttles: Smooth Airport Transfers: If you're flying in, think about employing airport shuttle services to get to your accommodation without a headache. The city core of Ajaccio may be reached by these shuttles in a quick and affordable manner from the airport.

9. Using Local Stores and Markets: Walking is frequently the most practical form of transportation when visiting the local markets, shops, and crafts in Ajaccio. Due to the city's small size and pedestrian-friendly districts, it is simple to go around on foot and you may explore markets and stores at your own pace.

10. Weather Considerations: - Adapt to Seasons: When making transportation arrangements, keep in mind that Corsica has varying weather patterns. While cooler months are better for exploring the hilly interior, summer may be ideal for beach drives and boat trips.

11. Language Considerations: - Basic French Knowledge: Although many residents, especially in tourist regions, understand English, knowing a few basic French phrases

might be useful, especially when utilizing public transit or asking for directions.

Finally, Ajaccio provides a beautiful selection of transportation choices, enabling you to customize your trip to your interests. These travel suggestions make sure that your discovery of Ajaccio and its surrounds is easy and memorable, whether you're driving through the Old Town, taking a beautiful route, or visiting adjacent islands.

Safety and Health

Traveling to Ajaccio, the crown gem of Corsica, offers the chance to focus your health as well as explore the island's breathtaking scenery and fascinating history. A seamless and pleasurable travel experience depends heavily on safety and health concerns. Here is a thorough guide on safety and health for visitors to Ajaccio, covering everything from navigating the city streets to delighting in local food.

General Safety Advice: Ajaccio, like any city, calls for some street smarts when navigating. Be mindful of your surroundings, particularly in busy locations and popular tourist destinations. Be mindful of pickpockets and safeguard your possessions, especially in crowded areas and on public transit.

Prepare yourself by becoming familiar with Ajaccio's emergency phone numbers. The emergency number in Europe is 112, and other emergency numbers include 15 for medical aid, 17 for police assistance, and 18 for fire services.

2. Health Warnings: Make sure you have adequate health insurance that covers medical costs and potential evacuation before departing for Ajaccio. Verify your insurance policy to see if it covers pursuits like water sports and hiking.

Check the requirements for any necessary vaccinations before to coming to Corsica. Regular vaccines must be current, and extra shots may be advised based on your travel plans.

Pharmacy: You may purchase over-the-counter medicines and essential medical supplies in Ajaccio's well-stocked pharmacies. Bring any essential medications and a prescription, if applicable, if you have special medical needs.

Safety around the water: Corsica's enticing seas may encourage you to go swimming, but always swim safely. If you are unfamiliar with the local currents, use approved swimming sites. Be mindful of rough shorelines and observe any written safety instructions.

Drink plenty of water because Ajaccio's Mediterranean environment tends to be heated, particularly in the summer. Drink lots of water to stay hydrated, especially if you're doing outside activities.

4. Dietary and Food Considerations: Culinary Adventures: For foodies, Ajaccio is a paradise, and getting to know Corsican cuisine is a thrill. Be wary about food safety, though. Select renowned eateries, and stay away from seafood that is uncooked or undercooked. When dining out, be explicit about any dietary restrictions or allergies you may have.

Drinking tap water in Ajaccio is normally safe, but if you're worried or have sensitive stomach, you might want to think about buying bottled water. If you want to trek or visit more isolated locations, be sure the water is safe to drink.

5. Sun Defense: Corsica has a Mediterranean climate, therefore you should wear sunscreen and other protective clothing throughout the summer. To protect yourself from the sun, use sunscreen with a high SPF, put on sunglasses, and think about wearing a wide-brimmed hat.

Practice heat safety by drinking plenty of water, finding cover from the sun when it's most intense, and clothing in layers. Plan outside activities during cooler times of the day if you intend to engage in them.

6. Outdoor Activities:

The mountains and trails that surround Ajaccio provide excellent hiking options. If you intend to trek, let someone know your plans, bring a map, and be prepared with the appropriate gear, including footwear and clothes. Inquire about the weather before leaving.

Water sports aficionados are welcomed by Ajaccio's seaside setting. If you're participating in sports like snorkeling, kayaking, or sailing, take safety precautions, use the proper equipment, and pay attention to the weather.

Local health care providers: Know the Location of the Nearest Hospital: Learn where the closest hospital or medical facility is in Ajaccio. Having this knowledge at your fingertips can help you save time in an emergency.

Pharmacies and Medical Assistance: Ajaccio pharmacies provide a variety of medical supplies. Pharmacists may frequently offer advice if you need medical assistance, and many of them can speak English.

Language Factors to Consider: Basic French Expressions: Although English is widely spoken in Ajaccio, especially in tourist areas, knowing a few basic French expressions might be useful, especially when asking for help in more local or non-touristy places.

In conclusion, visiting Ajaccio is a chance to emphasize safety and health in addition to being a sensory journey. You can make sure that your trip to Corsica is not only unforgettable but also secure and educational by being educated, taking the required measures, and adopting a conscientious attitude to your well-being.

CHAPTER 7: LANGUAGE AND COMMUNICATION

Useful Phrases

While English is understood in many tourist areas, making an effort to speak some basic French phrases in Ajaccio can greatly enhance your experience and interactions with locals. Corsicans often appreciate visitors who try to speak their language. Here's a handy guide of useful phrases to help you navigate Ajaccio:

Greetings and Basics:

1. *Hello:* Bonjour (bohn-zhoor)

2. *Good evening:* Bonsoir (bohn-swahr)

3. *Goodbye:* Au revoir (oh reh-vwahr)

4. *Please:* S'il vous plaît (seel voo pleh)

5. *Thank you:* Merci (mehr-see)

6. *Yes:* Oui (wee)

7. *No:* Non (nohn)

Common Courtesies:

8. *Excuse me / Sorry:* Excusez-moi (ehk-skew-zay mwah)

9. *I'm sorry:* Je suis désolé(e) (zhuh swee day-zoh-lay)

Asking for Information:

10. *Where is...?:* Où est... ? (oo eh...)

   11. *How much is this?:* Combien ça coûte ? (kohm-byen sah koot)
   12. *Can you help me?:* Pouvez-vous m'aider ? (poo-veh voo may-day)

Ordering Food and Drinks:

13. *I would like...:* Je voudrais... (zhuh voo-dray)

14. The menu, please: La carte, s'il vous plaît (lah kart, seel voo pleh)

15Water: Eau (oh)

16. Coffee: Café (kah-fay)

17. Wine: Vin (vah)

Getting Around:

18. Where is the train/bus station?: Où est la gare/l'arrêt de bus ? (oo eh lah gahr/lah-rey duh boo)

19. Taxi: Taxi (tak-see)

20. Airport: Aéroport (ah-ey-roh-por)

Numbers:

21. One: Un (uh)

22. *Two:* Deux (duh)

23. *Three:* Trois (twah)

24. *Four:* Quatre (kah-truh)

25. *Five:* Cinq (sank)

Emergencies:

26. *Help!:* Au secours ! (oh sek-oor)

27. *Police:* Police (poh-lees)

27. *Hospital:* Hôpital (oh-pee-tal)

28. *I need a doctor:* J'ai besoin d'un médecin (zhay boz-wah dun may-deh-sahn)

Shopping:

30. *How much does this cost?:* Combien ça coûte ? (kohm-byen sah koot)

31. *I want to buy...:* Je voudrais acheter... (zhuh voo-dray ah-shuh-tay)

Expressions of Appreciation:

32. *Beautiful:* Beau (boh)

33. Thank you very much: Merci beaucoup (mehr-see boh-koo)

Local Phrases:

34. *Corsica is beautiful:* La Corse est belle (lah kors eh bel)

Remember, the effort to speak a few phrases in French can go a long way in fostering positive interactions. Locals appreciate when visitors make an attempt to connect with their culture and language. Enjoy your time in Ajaccio, and bonne chance! (Good luck!)

CONCLUSION

You find yourself immersed in a tapestry of experiences as your voyage through Ajaccio, Corsica, comes to a conclusion, experiences that combine the island's natural beauty, rich history, and kind friendliness. The Corsican city of Ajaccio is more than just a place to visit; it's an experience with the heart of the Mediterranean, a mesmerizing kaleidoscope of cultures, landscapes, and customs that make a lasting impression on the tourist.

Ajaccio's attractiveness stems from its stunning natural surroundings as well as its historical significance as the birthplace of Napoleon Bonaparte. The city provides a symphony of scenery as it is tucked away between mountains and the Mediterranean Sea. Every view is a monument to Corsica's varied and pristine landscape, from the rough beauty of the Calanques de Piana to the beautiful beaches that edge the shore.

Historical resonance: With its old fortress, winding cobblestone alleyways, and Napoleon sculptures, Ajaccio wears its history with pride. When you explore the Old Town, you are taken back in time where the architecture and monuments reflect the fortitude of the Corsican people and Napoleon's legacy. Napoleon's birthplace, the Maison Bonaparte, serves as a live reminder of the city's historical significance.

Corsican cuisine, a combination of French and Italian influences, is a culinary delight that will take your taste buds on a voyage. The marketplaces of Ajaccio, such the thriving Central Market and the busy Fish Market, provide a glimpse into the culinary delights of the island. Every meal in Ajaccio is a celebration of Corsican culinary artistry, from the savory charcuterie and artisanal cheeses to the magnificent wines made from native grape varietals.

Warmth of Corsican Hospitality: The warmth of Corsican hospitality transforms Ajaccio from a location to an experience. Locals on the island are really kind and welcoming, proud of their unique culture. It doesn't matter if you're perusing artisanal shops, enjoying regional specialties at a family-run restaurant, or conversing with a market vendor—you can feel the real delight in sharing Corsica's riches.

Ajaccio is a fascinating city in and of itself, but it also acts as a starting point for seeing Corsica's more extensive beauties. Adventurers are encouraged to explore the island's numerous environments, which include mountains, woods, and stunning beaches. Travelers are enticed to explore Corsica's wild beauty by scenic roadways that take them to remote coves and hiking routes that provide panoramic views.

As your stay in Ajaccio draws to a conclusion, you come to the realization that it is difficult to adequately describe Corsica in words. It may be found in the perfume of the maquis brought by the sea air, in the polyphonic singing of Corsica that reverberates through the old streets, and in the warmth of the Mediterranean sun. In Ajaccio, you may go on a trip that goes beyond the tangible and transforms into a tapestry of memories, a collection of experiences that sum up Corsican life.

Finally, Ajaccio, Corsica, tells a story that goes beyond the commonplace and entices you to take part in it. It's a place that makes you feel connected to both the land and its history as well as the Corsican national spirit. Not only do you leave Ajaccio with mementos, but also with a tapestry of memories that will stay in your heart, luring you back to explore more of Corsica's enthralling stories.

Made in the USA
Las Vegas, NV
30 May 2024